CLASSIC
PASTA
SAUCES

CLASSIC
PASTA
SAUCES

RECIPES FOR THE QUICKEST, TASTIEST PASTA SAUCES

ELIZABETH MARTIN

SMITHMARK

ACKNOWLEDGEMENTS

The author and publishers would like to thank Kathryn Keegan for being the hand model and Viners (081-450 8900) for providing the saucepans. The photographs of Italy on pages 10, 22, 36, 54, 70 and 80 were reproduced with the permission of Carah Boden (copyright © Carah Boden).

This edition published in 1994 by
SMITHMARK Publishers Inc.
16 East 32nd Street
New York, NY 10016

SMITHMARK books are available for bulk purchase for sales promotion and premium use. For details write or call the manager of special sales, SMITHMARK Publishers Inc., 16 East 32nd Street, New York, NY 10016; (212) 532-6600.

© 1994 Anness Publishing Limited
1 Boundary Row
London SE1 8HP

Editorial Director: Joanna Lorenz
Project Editor: Clare Nicholson
Designer: David Rowley
Jacket Design: Peter Butler
Photographer: David Armstrong

ISBN 0-8317-1-1305-4

Typeset by MC Typeset Limited
Printed and bound in Singapore

Contents

Introduction

Pasta has always been the symbol of Italian food, and today delights the palates of many world wide.

It is probably the most versatile food and yet it is so simple, consisting of nothing more than a mixture of flour and water in its most basic form, or flour and egg, but it can be made in so many different shapes and served with a whole host of ingredients.

Pasta is now well known for being one of the healthiest natural foods, being low in fat and high in vitamins and carbohydrates. Served with plenty of vegetables and fish, it is a healthy part of a well-balanced diet. It is also very easy to digest, making it ideal for those with dietary problems. However, although pasta is in itself not fattening, it is wise to take note that the sauce it is served with will determine the calorific value of the whole dish.

In this book I have tried to create an array of sauces – some more complicated than others – to suit everyone. Most are so simple that they can be cooked in minutes, while a few need a little more preparation. But whichever you choose, remember, if you can't find any of the ingredients, then improvise, because I promise you anything is possible with pasta.

1 *tagliatelle*
2 *linguine*
3 *ravioli* **4** *pasta spirals (fusilli)*
5 *pasta tubes (rigatoni)* **6** *pasta shells (gomiti rigati)* **7** *tortellini*
8 *pasta ears (orecchiette)*
9 *spaghetti*
10 *penne* **11** *pasta twists (spirali)*
12 *pasta rounds (castiglioni)*
13 *spaghetti tricolore* **14** *curly spaghetti (fusilli col buco)* **15** *pasta spirals (fusilli tricolore)* **16** *short pasta tubes (canneroni)*
17 *macaroni*
18 *curly lasagne*

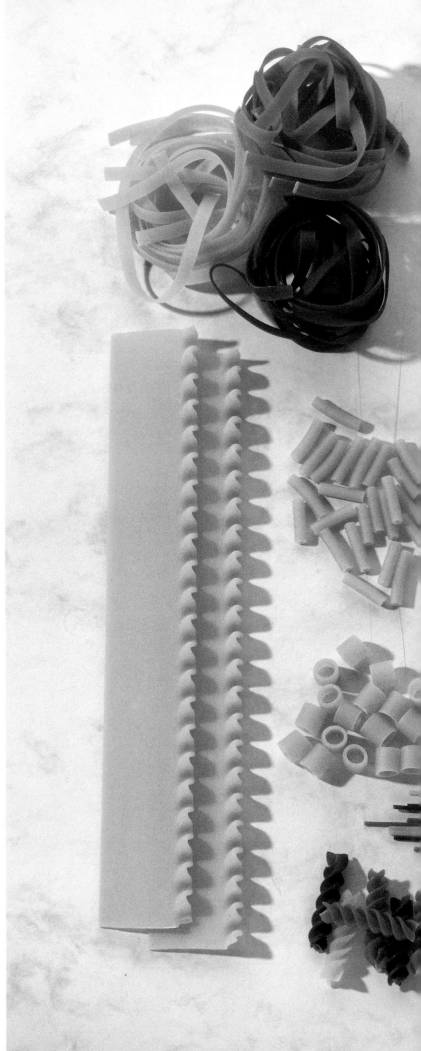

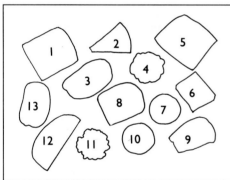

1 *Gruyère* 2 *dolcelatte* 3 *smoked mozzarella*
4 *mascarpone* 5 *Parmesan* 6 *fontina*
7 *herbed goats' cheese* 8 *Gouda* 9 *bel paese*
10 *mozzarella* 11 *curdled ricotta* 12 *Edam*
13 *roulé*

Choosing Pasta

There is an increasingly wide range of both fresh and dried pasta sold in supermarkets, as well as specialist shops and Italian delicatessens. Although none of these quite compare with fresh home-made pasta, they are still made with fine-quality ingredients.

Plain pasta – by far the most common – is made using durum flour and egg, but colored pasta does add interest to a meal: green pasta (*verde*) is flavoured with spinach and red pasta (*rosso*) with tomatoes. You can even buy black pasta flavoured with cuttlefish ink. Whole-wheat pasta is also available; it contains more fibre and consequently is more chewy in texture.

Illustrated on pages 6–7 are the shapes of pasta used in this book, with their names – however these vary simply because different regions of Italy have their own names for individual pasta shapes, as do the manufacturers.

There are no hard and fast rules on which pasta to use with which sauce, except that generally thin spaghetti suits the thinner sauces and shaped pastas suit the meatier sauces so that the bits get caught up in the pasta itself.

Cooking Pasta

Pasta is simple and easy to cook if you follow a few basic rules. It needs to be cooked in plenty of boiling water – allow 3¼ quarts water for each 450 g/ 1 lb of pasta.

1 Fill the pan with cold water and add about 1 tbsp of salt.

2 Bring to a rolling boil. Add a dash of olive oil.

3 Add the pasta and stir with a wooden spoon to separate the pasta.

4 Bring back to a rolling boil. Continue boiling, stirring occasionally, allowing 2–5 minutes for fresh pasta or 8–12 minutes for dried, until the pasta is *al dente*, which means firm to the bite. Pasta should not be mushy and should still hold its shape well. If you're not quite sure, continue boiling and keep checking regularly.

5 Drain and toss in the pasta sauce.

Choosing Herbs

Herbs are considered a very important part of Italian cooking, giving fragrant flavours to all types of pasta sauces.

When choosing herbs, look for those with unblemished leaves, that smell fresh and give off a pleasant scent when you break one. You can chop the leaves finely or coarsely, or leave them whole to stir into sauces.

Basil: one of Italy's most famous herbs. For the sweetest flavor, use freshly grown basil in a pot.

Cilantro: quite a strong flavor and looks like flat leaf parsley.

Dill: has a unique spicy, green taste. It goes well with fish, cream cheese and cucumber.

Oregano: a small-leaved herb with a delicate flavor, it is popular with Italian cooks.

Mint: a very common herb, this is used frequently in Italian cooking.

Parsley: popular in most cuisines, parsley is available as flat-leaved which has a better flavor than the more traditional curly variety.

Rosemary: gives a really strong Mediterranean taste.

Sage: an unforgettable flavor – quite powerful so use sparingly.

Thyme: the smallest leaved herb, it is extra pungent when fresh so use cautiously.

1 rosemary 2 sage 3 mint 4 cilantro 5 oregano 6 flat leaf parsley 7 basil 8 thyme 9 dill

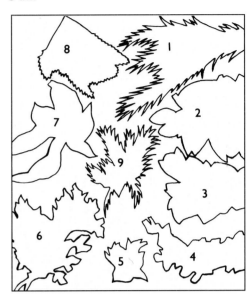

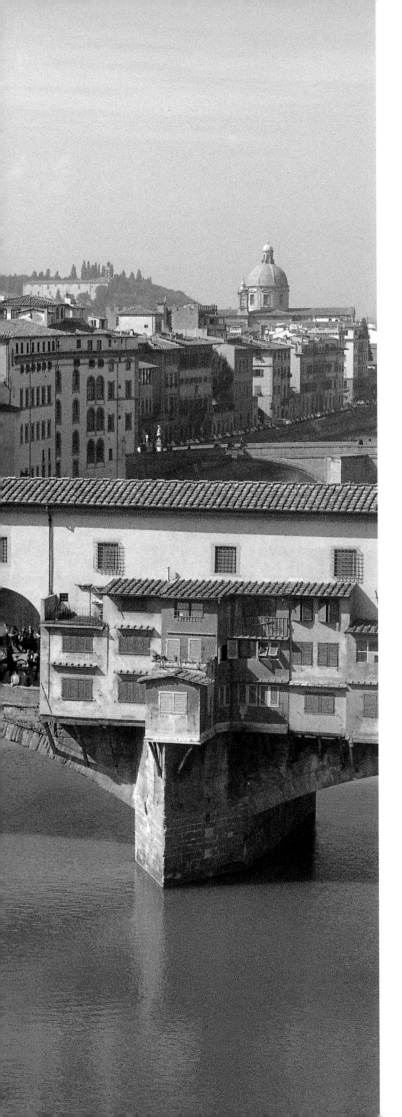

Traditional Sauces

This chapter is based on recipes, such as pesto sauce and carbonara, that conjure up the true taste of Italy. Obviously, the truly traditional recipes vary from region to region depending on the local ingredients, but I have chosen these sauces as they are real favorites everywhere.

Above   The Euganean hills, south of Padua, in spring.

Opposite   The Ponte Vecchio, Florence.

Ravioli with Four Cheese Sauce

This is a smooth cheese sauce that coats the pasta very evenly.

SERVES 4

INGREDIENTS
12 oz ravioli
¼ cup butter
½ cup plain flour
2 cups milk
2 oz Parmesan cheese
2 oz Edam cheese
2 oz Gruyère cheese
2 oz fontina cheese
salt and freshly ground black pepper
chopped fresh flat leaf parsley, to garnish

1 Cook the pasta following the instructions in the introduction.

2 ▲ Melt the butter in a saucepan, stir in the flour and cook for 2 minutes, stirring occasionally.

3 ▲ Gradually stir in the milk until well blended.

4 ▲ Bring the milk slowly to the boil, stirring constantly until thickened.

5 ▲ Grate the cheeses and stir them into the sauce. Stir until they are just beginning to melt. Remove from the heat and season.

6 ▲ Drain the pasta thoroughly and turn it into a large serving bowl. Pour over the sauce and toss to coat. Serve immediately, garnished with the chopped fresh parsley

COOK'S TIP

If you cannot find all of the above cheeses, simply substitute your favorites.

Spaghetti alla Carbonara

This is a light and creamy sauce flavored with bacon and lightly cooked eggs.

SERVES 4

INGREDIENTS
12 oz spaghetti
1 tbsp olive oil
1 onion, chopped
4 oz lean bacon or pancetta, rinded and diced
1 clove garlic, chopped
3 eggs
1¼ cups heavy cream
salt and freshly ground black pepper
2 oz Parmesan cheese
chopped fresh basil, to garnish

1 Cook the pasta following the instructions in the introduction.

2 ▲ Heat the oil in a frying pan and fry the onion and bacon for 10 minutes until softened. Stir in the garlic and fry for a further 2 minutes, stirring occasionally.

3 ▲ Meanwhile, beat the eggs in a bowl, then beat in the cream and seasoning. Grate the Parmesan cheese and stir into the cream mixture.

4 ▲ Stir the cream mixture into the onion and bacon and cook over a low heat for a few minutes, stirring constantly until heated through. Season to taste.

5 Drain the pasta thoroughly and turn it into a large serving bowl. Pour over the sauce and toss to coat. Serve immediately, garnished with chopped fresh basil.

COOK'S TIP

Italians would use pancetta which is lightly cured but similar to lean bacon. You can buy it in most supermarkets and delicatessens.

Pasta Twists with Classic Meat Sauce

This is a rich meat sauce which is ideal to serve with all types of pasta. The sauce definitely improves if kept overnight in the fridge. This allows the flavors time enough to mature.

SERVES 4

INGREDIENTS
1 lb ground beef
*4 oz hickory smoked bacon,
    chopped*
1 onion, chopped
2 stalks celery, chopped
1 tbsp plain flour
*²/₃ cup fresh or canned chicken stock or
    water*
3 tbsp/¹/₄ cup tomato purée
1 clove garlic, chopped
*3 tbsp chopped fresh mixed herbs, such as
    fresh oregano, parsley, marjoram,
    chives or use 1 tbsp dried mixed herbs
    instead*
1 tbsp red currant jelly
1 lb pasta twists (spirali)
salt and freshly ground black pepper
chopped oregano, to garnish

1 Heat a large saucepan and fry the beef and bacon for about 10 minutes, stirring occasionally until browned.

2 Add the onion and celery and cook for 2 minutes, stirring occasionally.

3 ▲ Stir in the flour and cook for 2 minutes, stirring constantly.

4 ▲ Pour in the stock or water and bring to a boil.

COOK'S TIP

The red currant jelly helps to draw out the flavour of the tomato purée. You can use a sweet mint jelly or chutney instead.

5 ▲ Stir in the tomato purée, garlic, herbs, red currant jelly and seasoning. Bring to a boil, cover and simmer for about 30 minutes, stirring occasionally.

6 Cook the pasta following the instructions in the introduction. Drain thoroughly and turn it into a large serving bowl. Pour the sauce over and toss to coat. Serve immediately, garnished with chopped fresh oregano.

Pasta Tubes with Meat and Cheese Sauce

These two sauces combine together to complement each other perfectly.

SERVES 4

INGREDIENTS

For the Meat Sauce
1 tbsp olive oil
12 oz ground beef
1 onion, chopped
1 clove garlic, chopped
14 oz can chopped tomatoes
1 tbsp dried mixed herbs
2 tbsp tomato purée

For the Cheese Sauce
¼ cup butter
½ cup plain flour
2 cups milk
2 egg yolks
⅓ cup Parmesan cheese, freshly grated
salt and freshly ground black pepper

12 oz ridged pasta tubes (rigatoni)
fresh basil sprigs, to garnish

I ▲ To make the meat sauce, heat the oil in a large frying pan and fry the beef for 10 minutes, stirring occasionally until browned. Add the onion and cook for 5 minutes, stirring occasionally.

2 ▲ Stir in the garlic, tomatoes, herbs and tomato purée. Bring to the boil, cover and simmer for 30 minutes.

3 ▲ Meanwhile, to make the cheese sauce, melt the butter in a small saucepan, then stir in the flour and cook for 2 minutes, stirring constantly.

4 Remove the pan from the heat and gradually stir in the milk. Return the pan to the heat and bring to the boil, stirring occasionally until thickened.

5 ▲ Add the egg yolks, cheese and seasoning and stir until well blended.

6 ▲ Preheat the oven on broil. Meanwhile, cook the pasta following the instructions in the introduction. Drain thoroughly and turn it into a large serving bowl. Pour the meat sauce over and toss to coat.

7 Divide the pasta among 4 ovenproof dishes. Spoon the cheese sauce over and place under the broiler until brown. Serve immediately garnished with fresh basil.

COOK'S TIP

Chopped canned tomatoes with added chopped herbs are now available from most supermarkets. If you prefer, simply substitute these and use half the quantity of dried herbs.

Curly Lasagne with Classic Tomato Sauce

A classic sauce that is simply delicious just served by itself.

SERVES 4

INGREDIENTS
2 tbsp olive oil
1 onion, chopped
2 tbsp tomato purée
1 tsp paprika
14 oz can chopped tomatoes, drained of
  juice
pinch of dried oregano
1¼ cups dry red wine
large pinch of sugar
salt and freshly ground black pepper
12 oz curly lasagne
Parmesan cheese shavings, to serve
chopped fresh flat leaf parsley, to garnish

1 ▲ Heat the oil in a large frying pan and fry the onion for 10 minutes, stirring occasionally until softened. Add the tomato purée and paprika and cook for 3 minutes.

2 ▲ Add the tomatoes, oregano, wine and sugar and season to taste, then bring to the boil.

3 ▲ Simmer for 20 minutes until the sauce has reduced and thickened, stirring occasionally.

4 Meanwhile, cook the pasta following the instructions in the introduction. Drain thoroughly and turn it into a large serving bowl. Pour the sauce over and toss to coat. Serve sprinkled with Parmesan cheese shavings and the chopped fresh parsley.

COOK'S TIP

If you cannot find curly lasagne use plain, snipped in half lengthways.

Pasta Spirals with Pesto Sauce

A light, fragrant sauce like this dish gives a temptingly different taste.

SERVES 4

INGREDIENTS
For the Pesto Sauce
2 oz fresh basil leaves without the stalks
2 garlic cloves, chopped
2 tbsp pine nuts
salt and freshly ground black pepper
²/₃ cup olive oil
¹/₃ cup Parmesan cheese, freshly grated

12 oz pasta spirals (fusilli)
freshly grated Parmesan cheese, to
    garnish
fresh basil sprigs, to garnish

1 Cook the pasta following the instructions in the introduction.

2 ▲ To make the pesto sauce, place the basil leaves, garlic, pine nuts, seasoning and olive oil in a food processor or blender. Blend until very creamy.

3 Transfer the mixture to a bowl and stir in the Parmesan cheese.

4 Drain the pasta thoroughly and turn it into a large bowl. Pour the sauce over and toss to coat. Divide among serving plates and serve, sprinkled with the extra Parmesan cheese and garnished with fresh basil.

COOK'S TIP

Fresh basil is widely available from most greengrocers and supermarkets, either in growing pots or packets. If you buy a plant, remove the flowers as they appear so the plant grows more leaves.

Pesto is best kept in a screw-topped jar in the fridge for up to 2 days. If you want to keep it a few days longer, cover the top with a thin layer of olive oil. This can be stirred into sauce when you are ready to add it to hot pasta.

Spaghetti with Meatballs

No Italian menu would be complete without meatballs. Serve these with a light green salad.

SERVES 4

INGREDIENTS
For the Meatballs
1 onion, chopped
1 garlic clove, chopped
12 oz ground lamb
1 egg yolk
1 tbsp dried mixed herbs
salt and freshly ground black pepper
1 tbsp olive oil

For the Sauce
1¼ cups tomato paste (see Cook's Tip)
2 tbsp chopped fresh basil
1 garlic clove, chopped
salt and freshly ground black pepper

12 oz spaghetti
fresh rosemary sprigs, to garnish
freshly grated Parmesan cheese,
*   to serve*

1 ▲ To make the meatballs, mix together the onion, clove of garlic, the lamb, egg yolk, herbs and seasoning until well blended.

2 ▲ Divide the mixture into 20 pieces and mold into balls. Place on a baking sheet, cover with plastic wrap and chill for 30 minutes.

3 ▲ Heat the oil in a large frying pan and place the meatballs in it.

4 ▲ Fry the meatballs for about 10 minutes, turning occasionally until browned.

5 ▲ Add the passata, basil, garlic and seasoning to the pan and bring to the boil. Cover and simmer for 20 minutes until the meatballs are tender.

6 Meanwhile, cook the pasta following the instructions in the introduction. Drain thoroughly and divide it among 4 serving plates. Spoon over meatballs and some of the sauce. Garnish each portion with a fresh rosemary sprig and serve immediately with plenty of freshly grated cheese.

COOK'S TIP

The tomato paste, called passata, is available in jars or cartons from Italian grocery stores and most supermarkets. It is made from sieved tomatoes, so if you cannot find any, drain and sieve canned tomatoes instead.

The meatballs can be made in advance. Place them on a baking sheet, cover with plastic wrap and chill for about 1 day.

Meat Sauces

The Italians, like most people, enjoy their meat dishes, particularly the sausages and salamis of which there are many very tasty local varieties. Used in a pasta sauce, meat adds a strong flavor and richness. When combining meat with pasta, follow the rule that a little meat goes a long way.

Above   The harbor at Lazise, Lake Garda.

Opposite   The Euganean hills, south of Padua.

Pasta Spirals with Chicken and Tomato Sauce

A recipe for a speedy supper – serve this dish with a mixed bean salad.

SERVES 4

INGREDIENTS
1 tbsp olive oil
1 onion, chopped
1 carrot, chopped
2 oz sun-dried tomatoes in olive oil,
    drained weight
1 garlic clove, chopped
14 oz can chopped tomatoes, drained
1 tbsp tomato paste
⅔ cup chicken stock
12 oz pasta spirals (fusilli)
8 oz boned chicken breast, diagonally
    sliced
salt and freshly ground black pepper
fresh mint sprigs, to garnish

I ▲ Heat the oil in a large frying pan and fry the onion and carrot for 5 minutes, stirring occasionally.

2 ▲ Chop the sun-dried tomatoes and set aside.

3 ▲ Stir the garlic, canned tomatoes, tomato paste and stock into the onions and carrots and bring to a boil. Simmer for 10 minutes, stirring occasionally.

4 Cook the pasta following the instructions in the introduction.

5 ▲ Pour the sauce into a food processor or blender and blend until smooth.

6 ▲ Return the sauce to the pan and stir in the sun-dried tomatoes and chicken. Bring back to the boil, then simmer for 10 minutes until the chicken is cooked. Adjust the seasoning.

7 ▲ Drain the pasta thoroughly and toss it in the sauce. Serve immediately, garnished with fresh mint.

COOK'S TIP

Sun-dried tomatoes are sold in jars soaked in vegetable or olive oil. The olive-oil soaked tomatoes do have a superior flavor. For extra flavor, fry the onion and carrot in 1 tbsp of the oil from the tomatoes.

Spaghetti with Bacon, Chili and Tomato Sauce

This substantial sauce is a meal in itself, so serve as a warming winter supper.

SERVES 4

INGREDIENTS
1 tbsp olive oil
8 oz hickory smoked bacon, coarsely chopped
12 oz spaghetti
1 tsp chili powder
1 quantity Classic Tomato Sauce (see Curly Lasagne with Classic Tomato Sauce)
salt and freshly ground black pepper
coarsely chopped fresh flat leaf parsley, to garnish

1 ▲ Heat the oil in a large frying pan and fry the bacon for about 10 minutes, until crisp and golden.

COOK'S TIP

To lower the calorie content of this sauce, pour off the fat in the frying pan at the end of step 2.

2 Cook the pasta following the instructions in the introduction.

3 ▲ Add the chili powder to the bacon and cook for 2 minutes. Stir in the tomato sauce and bring to the boil. Cover and simmer for 10 minutes. Season with salt and pepper.

4 Drain the pasta thoroughly and toss it with the sauce. Serve garnished with the chopped fresh parsley.

Tagliatelle with Pea and Ham Sauce

A colorful sauce, this is ideal served with crusty Italian or French bread.

SERVES 4

INGREDIENTS
12 oz tagliatelle
1 1/2 cups green peas, fresh or frozen
salt and freshly ground black pepper
1 1/4 cups light cream
1/3 cup fontina cheese, freshly grated
3 oz prosciutto, sliced into strips

1 Cook the pasta following the instructions in the introduction.

2 Plunge the peas into a pan of boiling salted water and cook for 7 minutes or until tender. Drain.

3 ▲ Place the cream and half the fontina cheese in a small saucepan and heat gently, stirring constantly until heated through.

4 ▲ Drain the pasta thoroughly and turn it into a large serving bowl. Toss together the pasta, prosciutto and peas and pour on the sauce. Add the remaining cheese and season with salt and pepper.

Spaghetti with Bacon, Chili and Tomato Sauce (top), and Tagliatelle with Pea and Ham Sauce (bottom).

Penne with Chicken and Ham Sauce

A meal in itself, this colorful pasta sauce is perfect for lunch or dinner.

SERVES 4

INGREDIENTS
12 oz penne
2 tbsp butter
1 onion, chopped
1 garlic clove, chopped
1 bay leaf
2 cups dry white wine
²/₃ cup crème fraîche
1¹/₂ cups cooked chicken, skinned, boned
  and diced
²/₃ cup cooked lean ham, diced
²/₃ cup Gouda cheese, grated
1 tbsp chopped fresh mint
salt and freshly ground black pepper
finely shredded fresh mint, to garnish

1 Cook the pasta following the instructions in the introduction.

2 ▲ Heat the butter in a large frying pan and fry the onion for 10 minutes until softened.

3 ▲ Add the garlic, bay leaf and wine and bring to the boil. Boil rapidly until reduced by half. Remove the bay leaf, then stir in the crème fraîche and return to the boil.

4 ▲ Add the chicken and ham and simmer for 5 minutes, stirring occasionally until heated through.

5 ▲ Add the cheese, mint and seasoning.

6 ▲ Drain the pasta thoroughly and turn it into a large serving bowl. Toss with the sauce immediately, garnished with shredded mint.

COOK'S TIP

Crème fraîche is a rich, full-fat French cream with a slightly acidic taste. If you can't find any, substitute sour cream.

Short Macaroni with Ham, Tomato and Oregano Sauce

SERVES 4

INGREDIENTS
12 oz short macaroni
3 tbsp olive oil
1 beefsteak tomato, chopped
1 garlic clove, chopped
1 cup cooked ham, cut into thick
 strips
1 cup goat cheese, diced
3 tbsp fresh oregano leaves
salt and freshly ground black pepper
goat cheese and torn fresh oregano,
 to garnish

I Cook the pasta following the instructions in the introduction.

2 ▲ Heat the oil in a large frying pan and fry the tomato, garlic and ham for 3 minutes.

COOK'S TIP

Goat cheese is available in many forms, such as in herbed oil, coated with coarsely ground pepper or plain.

3 ▲ Stir in the goat cheese and oregano and simmer for a further 30 seconds. Season to taste.

4 Drain the pasta thoroughly and toss it with the sauce. Serve immediately, garnished with extra goat cheese and fresh oregano.

Pasta 'Ears' with Pork in Mustard Sauce

The combination of pork and mustard give this sauce a real country taste.

SERVES 4

INGREDIENTS
12 oz pasta 'ears' (orecchiette)
4 tbsp olive oil
2 garlic cloves, chopped
12 oz pork fillet, thinly sliced
¼ cup butter
2½ cups flat mushrooms, sliced
1 tbsp wholegrain mustard
3 tbsp snipped fresh chives
salt and freshly ground black
 pepper
chopped fresh chives, to garnish

I Cook the pasta following the instructions in the introduction.

2 Heat the oil in large frying pan and fry the garlic and pork for 10 minutes, stirring occasionally until the pork is well browned and tender.

3 ▲ Add the butter, mushrooms and mustard and cook for 2 minutes, stirring occasionally. Add the chives and season to taste.

4 Meanwhile, drain the pasta thoroughly. Stir it into the pork mixture and cook for 1 minute until heated through. Serve immediately, garnished with fresh chives.

COOK'S TIP

To reduce the cost, use boneless pork chops, cut into strips.

Short Macaroni with Ham, Tomato and Oregano Sauce (top), and Pasta 'Ears' with Pork in Mustard Sauce (bottom).

Penne with Sausage and Parmesan Sauce

Spicy sausage tossed in this cheese and tomato sauce is delicious served on a bed of cooked pasta.

SERVES 4

INGREDIENTS
12 oz penne
1 lb ripe tomatoes
2 tbsp olive oil
8 oz chorizo sausage, diagonally
    sliced
1 garlic clove, chopped
2 tbsp chopped fresh flat leaf parsley
grated rind of 1 lemon
⅓ cup Parmesan cheese, freshly
    grated
salt and freshly ground black pepper
finely chopped fresh flat leaf parsley,
    to garnish

I Cook the pasta following the instructions in the introduction.

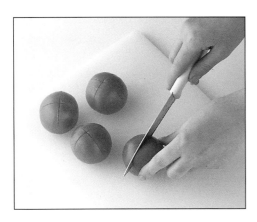

2 ▲ Slice the skins of the tomatoes with a knife, making a cross.

COOK'S TIP

Chorizo is quite a spicy Spanish pork sausage. A suitable Italian sausage would be salame napoletano, flavored with red and black pepper.

3 ▲ Place the tomatoes in a large bowl, cover with boiling water and leave to stand for 30 seconds.

4 ▲ Drain the tomatoes and peel off the skins.

5 ▲ Coarsely chop the tomatoes with a sharp knife.

6 ▲ Heat the oil in a frying pan and fry the sausage for 5 minutes, stirring occasionally until browned.

7 ▲ Add the tomatoes, garlic, parsley and grated lemon rind. Heat through, stirring, for 1 minute.

8 ▲ Add the Parmesan cheese and season to taste.

9 Drain the pasta thoroughly and toss it with the sauce to coat. Serve immediately, garnished with finely chopped fresh flat leaf parsley.

Tagliatelle with Chicken and Herb Sauce

This wine-flavored sauce is best served with green salad.

SERVES 4

INGREDIENTS
2 tbsp olive oil
1 red onion, cut into wedges
12 oz tagliatelle
1 garlic clove, chopped
2½ cups boned chicken breast, diced
1¼ cups dry vermouth
3 tbsp chopped fresh mixed herbs
⅔ cup ricotta
salt and freshly ground black pepper
shredded fresh mint, to garnish

1 ▲ Heat the oil in a large frying pan and fry the onion for 10 minutes until softened and the layers separate.

2 Cook the pasta following the instructions in the introduction.

3 ▲ Add the garlic and chicken to the pan and fry for 10 minutes, stirring occasionally until the chicken is browned all over and cooked through.

4 ▲ Pour in the vermouth, bring to the boil and boil rapidly until reduced by about half.

5 ▲ Stir in the herbs, ricotta and seasoning and heat through gently, but do not boil.

6 ▲ Drain the pasta thoroughly and toss it with the sauce to coat. Serve immediately, garnished with shredded fresh mint.

COOK'S TIP

If you don't want to use vermouth, use dry white wine instead. Orvieto and Frascati are two Italian wines that are ideal to use in this sauce.

Vegetable Sauces

Throughout the year in Italy, markets display an abundance of different vegetables of which the Italians make full use in their pasta dishes. The key to delicious vegetable sauces is to use really fresh produce which is full of flavor. Be adventurous with your choice of ingredients and adapt the recipes, selecting vegetables as they come into season.

Above   A vegetable stall in Padua market.

Opposite   A market scene in the Piazza dell' Erbe, Padua.

Spaghetti with Ratatouille Sauce

This is ideal to serve for vegetarians and makes a delicious alternative to any meat or fish dish.

SERVES 4

INGREDIENTS
2 tbsp olive oil
1 onion, sliced
1 clove garlic, chopped
1½ cups zucchini, sliced
1½ cups eggplant, halved lengthways and cut into large chunks
2 tbsp tomato paste
14 oz can chopped tomatoes
2 tbsp chopped fresh mixed herbs, such as parsley, basil, oregano
salt and freshly ground black pepper
12 oz spaghetti
fresh flat leaf parsley sprigs, to garnish
freshly grated Parmesan cheese, to serve

1 ▲ Heat the oil in a large saucepan and fry the onion for 5 minutes. Add the garlic, zucchini and eggplant and cook for 2 minutes, stirring occasionally.

COOK'S TIP

For extra color and flavor, add sliced orange pepper when cooking the onion.

2 ▲ Stir in the tomato paste, tomatoes, herbs and seasoning and bring to a boil. Simmer for about 20–30 minutes until thickened, stirring occasionally.

3 Meanwhile, cook the pasta following the instructions in the introduction. Drain thoroughly and stir it with the sauce. Toss to coat and garnish with fresh flat leaf parsley. Serve with plenty of freshly grated Parmesan cheese.

Spaghetti with Pepper and Tomato Sauce

SERVES 4

INGREDIENTS
12 oz spaghetti
2 tbsp olive oil
2 onions, chopped
1 red pepper, cored, seeded and cut into strips
1 green pepper, cored, seeded and cut into strips
1 yellow pepper, cored, seeded and cut into strips
3 tomatoes, skinned, seeded and chopped
1 garlic clove, chopped
1 tbsp chopped fresh oregano
fresh oregano sprigs, to garnish
salt and freshly ground black pepper

1 Cook the pasta following the instructions in the introduction.

2 Heat the oil in a large frying pan and fry the onions and peppers for 10 minutes until softened.

3 ▲ Stir in the tomatoes, garlic, oregano and seasoning and bring to the boil. Cover and simmer for 2 minutes.

4 Drain the pasta thoroughly and toss it with the sauce. Serve immediately, garnished with fresh oregano.

COOK'S TIP

For an even quicker sauce, use already cut pepper strips that you can buy in jars of olive oil. Fry the onion for 3–5 minutes in step 2, then drain the peppers and add them in step 3.

Spaghetti with Ratatouille Sauce (top), and Spaghetti with Pepper and Tomato Sauce (bottom).

Spaghetti with Mixed Mushroom and Basil Sauce

The combination of mixed mushroom and freshly chopped sweet basil tossed with spaghetti is well complemented by tomato salad.

SERVES 4

INGREDIENTS
1/4 cup butter
1 onion, chopped
12 oz spaghetti
5 cups mixed mushrooms, such as cremini and button, sliced
1 garlic clove, chopped
1 1/4 cups sour cream
2 tbsp chopped fresh basil
1/3 cup Parmesan cheese, freshly grated
salt and freshly ground black pepper
torn flat leaf parsley, to garnish
freshly grated Parmesan cheese, to serve

1 Melt the butter in a large frying pan and fry the onion for 10 minutes until softened.

2 Cook the pasta following the instructions in the introduction.

3 ▲ Stir the mushrooms and garlic into the onion mixture and fry for 10 minutes until softened.

4 ▲ Add the sour cream, basil, Parmesan cheese and seasoning. Cover and heat through.

5 Drain the pasta thoroughly and toss it with the sauce and garnish with torn flat leaf parsley. Serve immediately with plenty of Parmesan cheese.

Tagliatelle with Spring Vegetable Sauce

Adapt this recipe to suit your own taste. Select a combination of the vegetables recommended in the ingredients list, amounting to 12 oz in total. The rosemary will give a very Mediterranean flavor to the vegetables.

SERVES 4

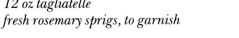

INGREDIENTS
2 tbsp olive oil
4 oz baby carrots, halved lengthways
4 oz baby eggplant, halved lengthways
4 oz baby zucchini, halved lengthways
4 oz patty pan squashes (alternative)
4 oz snow peas (alternative)
4 oz baby turnips, halved (alternative)
4 oz baby sweetcorn (alternative)
2 garlic cloves, chopped
1 tbsp chopped fresh rosemary
1¼ cups light cream
salt and freshly ground black pepper
12 oz tagliatelle
fresh rosemary sprigs, to garnish

1 ▲ Heat the oil in a large frying pan and fry the vegetables, garlic and rosemary, covered over a gentle heat, for 30 minutes until browned, stirring twice during cooking.

2 ▲ Remove from the heat and stir in the cream, scraping any sediment from the base of the pan. Season to taste. Return to the heat and cook for a further 4 minutes until heated through.

3 Meanwhile, cook the pasta following the instructions in the introduction.

4 Drain the pasta thoroughly and stir it into the vegetables. Serve immediately, garnished with fresh rosemary.

COOK'S TIP

Baby vegetables are available from most good greengrocers and larger supermarkets.

If you can't find any fresh rosemary, substitute ½ tbsp of dried.

Curly Spaghetti with Walnut and Cream Sauce

A classic Italian sauce with a strong, nutty flavour, this should be served with delicately flavored salad.

SERVES 4

INGREDIENTS
12 oz curly spaghetti (fusilli col buco)
1/2 cup walnut halves
2 tbsp butter
1 1/4 cups milk
1 cup fresh breadcrumbs
*2 tbsp Parmesan cheese, freshly
   grated*
2 tbsp Cheddar cheese, grated
pinch of freshly grated nutmeg
salt and freshly ground black pepper
fresh rosemary sprigs, to garnish

1 Cook the pasta following the instructions in the introduction. Meanwhile, preheat the broiler.

2 ▲ Spread the walnuts evenly over the broiling pan. Broil for about 5 minutes, turning them over occasionally until evenly toasted.

COOK'S TIP

Toasted walnuts add a lovely flavor to this unusual sauce, but if you prefer you can use pecans as an alternative.

3 ▲ Remove from the heat, place in a clean dish cloth and rub away the skins.

4 ▲ Roughly chop the nuts.

5 ▲ Heat the butter and milk in a saucepan until the butter is melted.

6 ▲ Stir in the breadcrumbs and nuts and heat gently for 2 minutes, stirring constantly until thickened.

7 ▲ Add the Parmesan and Cheddar cheese, nutmeg and seasoning to taste.

8 ▲ Drain the pasta thoroughly and toss it in the sauce. Serve immediately, garnished with fresh rosemary.

Spaghetti with Pesto, Shallot and Olive Sauce

SERVES 4

INGREDIENTS
12 oz spaghetti
2 tbsp olive oil
1½ cups small shallots, halved
1 quantity Pesto Sauce (see Pasta Spirals
 with Pesto Sauce)
1 cup pitted black olives, halved
salt and freshly ground black pepper
torn fresh basil, to garnish

COOK'S TIP

If you make your own pesto it will keep for 2 days in the refrigerator.

1 ▲ Heat the oil in a frying pan and fry the shallots for 10 minutes until browned. Cover the pan and cook for 10 minutes over a gentle heat until softened.

2 Meanwhile, cook the pasta following the instructions in the introduction.

3 ▲ Stir the pesto sauce, olives and seasoning into the shallots.

4 Drain the pasta thoroughly and toss it in the sauce to coat. Serve immediately, garnished with fresh oregano leaves.

Penne with Zucchini and Goat Cheese Sauce

SERVES 4

INGREDIENTS
12 oz penne
4 tbsp olive oil
2 garlic cloves, chopped
2 cups zucchini, sliced
1⅓ cups herbed goat cheese, diced
2 tbsp chopped fresh oregano
salt and freshly ground black
 pepper
shredded oregano, to garnish

COOK'S TIP

Diced feta cheese, with its sharp, salty taste, is a good alternative for goat cheese. Only buy feta cheese that is bright white with a crumbly texture.

1 Cook the pasta following the instructions in the introduction.

2 ▲ Heat the oil in a large frying pan and cook the garlic and zucchini over a gentle heat for 10 minutes, stirring occasionally.

3 ▲ Add the goat cheese and oregano and cook for 1 minute until heated through.

4 Drain the pasta thoroughly and stir it into the sauce. Serve immediately, garnished with flat leaf parsley.

Spaghetti with Pesto, Shallot and Olive Sauce (top), and Penne with Zucchini and Goat Cheese Sauce (bottom).

Tagliatelle with Mozzarella and Asparagus Sauce

This attractive sauce is best served with a leafy red salad.

SERVES 4

INGREDIENTS
8 oz asparagus tips
12 oz tagliatelle
½ cup butter
1 onion, chopped
1 garlic clove, chopped
2 tbsp chicken stock or water
⅔ cup heavy cream
½ cup mozzarella cheese, grated
salt and freshly ground black pepper
fresh flat leaf parsley sprigs, to garnish

I ▲ Plunge the asparagus into a pan of boiling salted water and cook for 5–10 minutes until tender. Drain.

2 Cook the pasta following the instructions in the introduction.

3 ▲ Melt the butter in a large frying pan and fry the onion for 5 minutes until softened.

4 ▲ Stir in the asparagus, garlic and chicken stock or water.

5 ▲ Stir in the cream and bring to a boil. Simmer for 2 minutes, stirring occasionally.

6 ▲ Add the mozzarella cheese and simmer for 1 minute until melted. Season to taste.

7 ▲ Drain the pasta thoroughly and toss it in the sauce to coat. Serve immediately, garnished with flat leaf parsley sprigs.

COOK'S TIP

Fresh asparagus is still quite seasonal, therefore keep your eyes open and cook them in this delicious sauce when they are at their best. If you are in a hurry, use canned asparagus tips instead of fresh. Drain them well and add them in step 6.

Pasta Spirals with Mascarpone and Spinach Sauce

This creamy, green sauce tossed in lightly cooked pasta is best served with sun-dried tomato ciabatta bread.

SERVES 4

INGREDIENTS
12 oz pasta spirals (fusilli)
1/4 cup butter
1 onion, chopped
1 garlic clove, chopped
2 tbsp fresh thyme leaves
8 oz frozen spinach leaves, thawed
salt and freshly ground black pepper
1 1/4 cups mascarpone cheese
fresh thyme sprigs, to garnish

1 Cook the pasta following the instructions in the introduction.

2 ▲ Melt the butter in a large saucepan and fry the onion for 10 minutes until softened.

3 ▲ Stir in the garlic, thyme, spinach and seasoning and heat gently for about 5 minutes, stirring occasionally until heated through.

4 ▲ Stir in the mascarpone cheese and heat gently until heated through.

5 Drain the pasta thoroughly and stir it into the sauce. Toss until well coated. Serve immediately, garnished with fresh thyme.

COOK'S TIP

Mascarpone is a rich Italian cream cheese. If you cannot find any, use ordinary cream cheese instead.

Macaroni with Hazelnut and Coriander Sauce

This is a variation on pesto sauce, giving a smooth, herby flavor of coriander.

SERVES 4

INGREDIENTS
12 oz macaroni
1/3 cup shelled hazelnuts, skinned
2 garlic cloves
1 bunch fresh coriander
1 tsp salt
6 tbsp/1/4 cup olive oil
fresh coriander sprigs, to garnish

1 Cook the pasta following the instructions in the introduction.

2 ▲ Meanwhile, finely chop the nuts.

3 ▲ Place the nuts and remaining ingredients, except 1 tbsp of the oil, in a food processor or pestle and mortar and grind together to create the sauce.

4 ▲ Heat the remaining oil in a saucepan and add the sauce. Fry very gently for about 1 minute until heated through.

5 Drain the pasta thoroughly and stir it into the sauce. Toss well to coat. Serve immediately, garnished with fresh coriander.

COOK'S TIP

To remove the skins from the hazelnuts, place them in a 350°F oven for 20 minutes, then rub off the skins with a clean dish-towel.

Tagliatelle with Mixed Vegetables and Orange Sauce

This colorful sauce is delicious served with large amounts of freshly grated Parmesan cheese.

SERVES 4

INGREDIENTS
1/4 cup butter
2 tbsp olive oil
2 leeks, thickly sliced
12 oz tagliatelle
2/3 cup peas, thawed if frozen
4 oz asparagus tips
1 tbsp plain flour
grated rind and juice of 1 orange
2/3 cup orange juice
salt and freshly ground black pepper

1 ▲ Melt the butter with the oil in a frying pan and fry the leeks for 5–10 minutes until almost softened.

2 Cook the pasta following the instructions in the introduction.

3 ▲ Stir the peas and asparagus into the leeks, cover and simmer for about 5 minutes until just softened.

4 ▲ Add the flour and cook, stirring occasionally, for about 1 minute.

5 ▲ Gradually stir in the grated rind and orange juices. Return the pan to the heat and bring slowly to the boil, stirring constantly until thickened.

6 ▲ Drain the pasta thoroughly and stir it into the sauce. Toss to coat, season to taste and serve immediately.

COOK'S TIP

Other types of pasta that would be suitable for this sauce include fettucine which is thinner and pappardelle which is thicker.

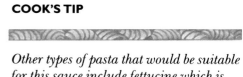

Pasta Twists with Sun-dried Tomato Sauce

Sun-dried tomatoes give this sauce a truly authentic Mediterranean taste. Serve with freshly baked rolls.

SERVES 4

INGREDIENTS

12 oz pasta twists (spirali)
2 tbsp olive oil
1 red onion, thinly sliced
2 garlic cloves, chopped
7 oz jar sun-dried tomatoes in oil, drained
2 tbsp coarsely chopped fresh herbs
14 oz can chopped tomatoes
¼ cup cream cheese
salt and freshly ground black pepper
chopped fresh flat leaf parsley, to garnish

1 Cook the pasta following the instructions in the introduction.

2 ▲ Heat the oil in a frying pan and cook the onion for 5 minutes until slightly softened.

3 ▲ Add the garlic and sun-dried tomatoes and stir well.

4 ▲ Add the herbs and tomatoes and bring to the boil. Simmer for 5 minutes until sauce has thickened.

5 Drain the pasta thoroughly, set aside and keep it warm.

6 ▲ Stir the cream cheese and seasoning into the sauce and return to the boil, stirring constantly until well blended.

7 ▲ Add the pasta to the sauce, toss it to coat and serve immediately, garnished with chopped flat leaf parsley.

COOK'S TIP

Use any combination of mixed herbs. Fresh basil, flat leaf parsley and oregano will add an authentic flavor. Chives will also complement the sun-dried tomatoes.

Cut the cost of using sun-dried tomatoes in oil. Buy a large bag of dry sun-dried tomatoes from a health-food shop. Leave the tomatoes to soak overnight in water. Squeeze out the excess moisture, then put in a jar and cover with virgin olive oil. Add sliced garlic and fresh herbs for extra flavor. These will keep for several months, covered in the refrigerator.

Fish & Seafood Sauces

Completely surrounded by sea, apart from the northern part, and with well-stocked lakes, rivers and streams, it is not surprising that fish and seafood are regarded as staple foodstuffs in Italy. Fish and seafood are the perfect partner for pasta and they often make quick, simple and nutritious sauces suitable for any occasion.

Above   The fish market in Chioggia, Veneto

Opposite   The harbor at Chioggia, Veneto.

Pasta Tubes with Tuna and Olive Sauce

A colorful Italian-style sauce, this combines well with a thicker and shorter pasta.

SERVES 4

INGREDIENTS
12 oz pasta tubes (rigatoni)
2 tbsp olive oil
1 onion, chopped
2 garlic cloves, chopped
14 oz can chopped tomatoes
4 tbsp tomato paste
salt and freshly ground black pepper
8 oz can tuna in oil, drained and
    flaked
1/2 tsp anchovy paste
1/3 cup pitted black olives,
    quartered
1 tbsp chopped fresh oregano
1 tbsp capers, rinsed
2/3 cup Cheddar cheese, grated
3 tbsp fresh white breadcrumbs
flat leaf parsley sprigs, to garnish

1 Cook the pasta following the instructions in the introduction.

2 ▲ Meanwhile, heat the oil in a frying pan and fry the onion and garlic for about 10 minutes until softened.

3 ▲ Add the tomatoes, tomato paste and seasoning and bring to the boil. Simmer gently for 5 minutes stirring occasionally.

4 ▲ Stir in the tuna, anchovy paste, olives, oregano and capers. Spoon the mixture into a serving dish.

5 ▲ Drain the pasta thoroughly and toss it well in the sauce and spoon it into flameproof serving bowls.

6 ▲ Preheat the broiler and sprinkle the cheese and breadcrumbs over the pasta. Broil for about 10 minutes until the pasta is heated through and the cheese has melted. Serve immediately, garnished with flat leaf parsley.

COOK'S TIP

This speedy sauce is ideal to make when guests drop in unexpectedly because most of the ingredients are standard kitchen cupboard items. Unopened olives packed in brine will keep for about one year.

Spaghetti with Monkfish

A truly Chinese spicy taste is what makes this sauce so different.

SERVES 4

INGREDIENTS
12 oz spaghetti
1 lb monkfish, skinned
8 oz zucchini
1 green chilli, cored and seeded (optional)
1 tbsp olive oil
1 large onion, chopped
1 tsp turmeric
²/₃ cup shelled peas, thawed if frozen
2 tsp lemon juice
5 tbsp hoisin sauce
²/₃ cup water
salt and freshly ground black pepper
a sprig of dill, to garnish

I Cook the pasta following the instructions in the introduction.

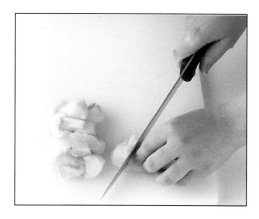

2 ▲ With a knife, cut the monkfish into bite-size pieces.

3 ▲ Thinly slice the zucchini, then finely chop the chili.

4 ▲ Heat the oil in a large frying pan and fry the onion for 5 minutes until softened. Add the turmeric.

5 ▲ Add the chili, zucchini and peas and fry over a medium heat for about 5 minutes until the vegetables have softened.

6 ▲ Stir in the fish, lemon juice, hoisin sauce and water. Bring to a boil, then simmer, uncovered, for about 5 minutes or until the fish is tender. Season to taste.

7 ▲ Drain the pasta thoroughly and turn it into a serving bowl. Toss in the sauce to coat. Serve immediately, garnished with fresh dill.

COOK'S TIP

This dish is quite low in calories, therefore ideal for dieters. Hoisin sauce is widely available from most supermarkets or Chinese stores.

Tagliatelle with Avocado, Tomato and Haddock Sauce

You will need to start this recipe the day before because the haddock should be left to marinate overnight.

SERVES 4

INGREDIENTS
12 oz fresh haddock fillets, skinned
1/2 tsp each ground cumin, ground
    coriander and turmeric
salt and freshly ground black pepper
2/3 cup cream cheese
2/3 cup heavy cream
1 tbsp lemon juice
2 tbsp butter
1 onion, chopped
1 tbsp plain flour
2/3 cup fish stock
12 oz tagliatelle
1 avocado, peeled, pitted and sliced
2 tomatoes, seeded and chopped
fresh rosemary sprigs, to garnish

I ▲ Carefully cut the haddock into bite-size pieces.

2 ▲ Mix together the spices, seasoning, cream cheese, cream and lemon juice.

3 ▲ Stir in the haddock to coat. Cover and leave to marinate overnight.

4 ▲ Heat the butter in a frying pan and fry the onion for about 10 minutes until softened. Stir in the flour, then blend in the stock until smooth.

5 ▲ Carefully stir in the haddock mixture until well blended. Bring to a boil, stirring, cover and simmer for about 30 seconds.

6 Meanwhile, cook the pasta following the instructions in the introduction.

7 ▲ Stir the avocado and tomatoes into the haddock mixture.

8 Drain the pasta thoroughly and divide it between serving plates. Spoon over the sauce and serve immediately, garnished with fresh rosemary.

COOK'S TIP

Cod and monkfish are tasty alternatives to haddock. You can also combine half fresh haddock and half smoked haddock.

Seafood Spaghetti

This sauce offers a fresh ocean flavor. Serve with hunks of crusty French bread.

SERVES 4

INGREDIENTS
12 oz spaghetti
¼ cup butter
1 onion, chopped
1 red pepper, cored, seeded and coarsely chopped
2 garlic cloves, chopped
1 tbsp paprika
1 lb fresh mussels
⅔ cup dry white wine
2 tbsp chopped fresh parsley
8 oz peeled shrimp
⅔ cup crème fraîche
salt and freshly ground black pepper
finely chopped fresh flat leaf parsley, to garnish

I   Cook the pasta following the instructions in the introduction.

2 ▲ Melt the butter in a frying pan and fry the onion, pepper, garlic and paprika for 5 minutes until almost softened.

3 ▲ Rinse and scrub the mussels, making sure all the shells are tightly shut and, if not, close when tapped sharply with the back of a knife. Discard any open shells.

4 ▲ Add the wine to the pan and bring to the boil.

5 ▲ Stir in the mussels and parsley, cover and simmer for about 5 minutes until the mussels have opened. Discard any mussels that remain closed.

6 ▲ Remove the mussels from the pan and keep warm. Add the shrimp, bring the juices back to the boil and boil rapidly until reduced by half.

7 ▲ Stir in the crème fraîche until well blended. Season to taste. Return the fish to the pan and simmer for 1 minute to heat through.

8   Drain the pasta thoroughly and divide it among the serving plates. Spoon over the shellfish and serve, garnished with finely chopped fresh flat leaf parsley.

COOK'S TIP

You can buy mixed seafood in supermarkets. Simply substitute for the mixed shellfish.

Linguine with Clam, Leek and Tomato Sauce

Toss together this sauce for a real seafood flavor and serve with a light mixed salad. Canned clams make this a speedy sauce for those in a real hurry.

SERVES 4

INGREDIENTS
12 oz linguine
2 tbsp butter
2 leeks, thinly sliced
⅔ cup dry white wine
4 tomatoes, skinned, seeded and chopped
pinch of ground turmeric (optional)
9 oz can clams, drained
2 tbsp chopped fresh basil
4 tbsp crème fraîche
salt and freshly ground black pepper

1 Cook the pasta following the instructions in the introduction.

2 ▲ Meanwhile, melt the butter in a small saucepan and fry the leeks for about 5 minutes until softened.

3 Add the wine, tomatoes and turmeric, bring to the boil and boil until reduced by half.

4 ▲ Stir in the clams, basil, crème fraîche and seasoning and heat through gently without boiling.

5 Drain the pasta thoroughly and toss it in the sauce. Serve immediately.

Macaroni with Jumbo Shrimp, Ham and Parsley Sauce

SERVES 4

INGREDIENTS
12 oz short macaroni
3 tbsp olive oil
12 shelled raw jumbo shrimp
1 garlic clove, chopped
1 cup smoked ham, diced
⅔ cup red wine
½ small radicchio lettuce, shredded
2 egg yolks, beaten
2 tbsp chopped fresh flat leaf parsley
⅔ cup heavy cream
salt and freshly ground black pepper
shredded fresh basil, to garnish

1 Cook the pasta following the instructions in the introduction.

2 Meanwhile, heat the oil in a frying pan and cook the shrimp, garlic and ham for 5 minutes, stirring occasionally until the shrimp are tender.

3 ▲ Add the wine and radicchio, bring to the boil and boil rapidly until the juices are reduced by half.

COOK'S TIP

Flat leaf parsley is a pretty herb with more flavor than the curly variety. If you buy a large bunch, finely chop the leftover parsley and freeze it in a small plastic bag. It is then ready to sprinkle onto bubbling soups or casseroles as a garnish.

4 ▲ Stir in the egg yolks, parsley and cream and bring almost to the boil, stirring constantly, then simmer until the sauce thickens slightly. Adjust the seasoning to taste.

5 Drain pasta thoroughly and toss it in the sauce to coat. Serve immediately, garnished with shredded fresh basil.

Thin Noodles with Clam, Leek and Tomato Sauce (top), and Macaroni with Jumbo Shrimp, Ham and Parsley Sauce (bottom).

Stir-fried Vegetable and Shrimp Sauce with Curly Spaghetti

You will need to start this recipe the day before because the shrimp should be left to marinate overnight.

SERVES 4

INGREDIENTS
1 lb peeled shrimp
4 tbsp/¹/₃ cup soy sauce
3 tbsp olive oil
12 oz curly spaghetti (fusilli col buco)
1 yellow pepper, cored, seeded and cut into strips
1¹/₂ cups broccoli florets
1 bunch scallions, shredded
1 in piece fresh ginger root, peeled and shredded
1 tbsp chopped fresh oregano
2 tbsp dry sherry
1 tbsp cornstarch
1¹/₄ cups fish stock
salt and freshly ground black pepper

I ▲ Place the shrimp in a mixing bowl. Stir in half the soy sauce and 2 tbsp of the olive oil. Cover and marinate overnight.

2 Cook the pasta following the instructions in the introduction.

3 ▲ Meanwhile, heat the remaining oil in a wok or frying pan and fry the shrimp for 1 minute.

4 ▲ Add the pepper, broccoli, scallions, ginger and oregano and stir-fry for 1–2 minutes.

5 ▲ Drain the pasta thoroughly and set it aside and keep warm. Meanwhile, blend together the sherry and cornstarch until smooth. Stir in the stock and remaining soy sauce until well blended.

6 ▲ Pour the sauce into the wok or pan, bring to the boil and stir-fry for 2 minutes until the sauce has thickened.

7 ▲ Turn the pasta into a serving bowl, pour over the sauce and toss to coat. Season to taste. Serve immediately.

COOK'S TIP

If you cannot find curly spaghetti, use other thin, long pasta such as linguine or bucatini, which looks like spaghetti but has a hole running through the center of it.

Spaghetti with Mixed Shellfish Sauce

A special occasion sauce for an evening of entertaining is just what this is, so serve it in bountiful portions.

SERVES 4

INGREDIENTS
1/4 *cup butter*
2 shallots, chopped
2 garlic cloves, chopped
12 oz spaghetti
2 tbsp finely chopped fresh basil
1 1/4 *cups dry white wine*
1 lb mussels, scrubbed and debearded
4 oz squid, cleaned
12 oz raw peeled shrimp
1 tsp chili powder
2/3 *cup sour cream*
salt and freshly ground black pepper
1/3 *cup Parmesan cheese, freshly grated*
chopped fresh flat leaf parsley, to garnish

1 ▲ Melt half the butter in a frying pan and fry 1 shallot and 1 garlic clove for 5 minutes until softened.

2 Cook the pasta following the instructions in the introduction.

3 ▲ Stir in half the basil and the wine and bring to the boil.

4 ▲ Discard any mussels that are open and do not shut when tapped with the back of a knife. Quickly add the remaining mussels to the pan, cover and simmer for about 5 minutes until all the shells have opened. Discard any mussels that do not open. Using a slotted spoon, transfer the mussels to a plate, remove them from their shells and return to the pan. Reserve a few mussels in the shells for garnishing.

5 Meanwhile, slice the squid into thin circles. Melt the remaining butter in a frying pan and fry the remaining shallot and garlic for about 5 minutes until softened.

6 ▲ Add the remaining basil, the squid, chili powder and shrimp to the pan and stir-fry for 5 minutes until the prawns have turned pink and tender.

7 ▲ Turn the mussel mixture into the shrimp mixture and bring to a boil. Stir in the sour cream and season to taste. Simmer for 1 minute.

8 Drain the pasta thoroughly and stir it into the sauce with the Parmesan cheese until well coated. Serve immediately, garnished with chopped flat leaf parsley and the reserved mussels in their shells.

COOK'S TIP

Take care that the shrimp and squid do not over-cook or they will become rubbery.

Cheese Sauces

By far the simplest way to serve pasta is with a generous grating of Parmesan cheese and olive oil, but cheeses are enjoyed throughout Italy and there are many delicious country specialities. The unusual cheeses, made locally by farmers, are rarely seen outside Italy but it is becoming increasingly easy to obtain the better-known varieties in good delicatessens and supermarkets.

Above   The cheese market in Padua.

Opposite   The Pustertal Valley, the Italian Dolomites.

Tortellini with Mushroom and Three Cheese Sauce

SERVES 4

INGREDIENTS

*1 lb ricotta-and-spinach filled ortellini
tortellini*
¼ cup butter
2 garlic cloves, chopped
*3 cups field or button mushrooms,
sliced*
1 tbsp plain flour
¾ cup milk
*⅓ cup Parmesan cheese, freshly
grated*
⅓ cup fontina cheese, grated
⅔ cup ricotta cheese
4 tbsp/⅓ cup light cream
2 tbsp snipped fresh chives
salt and freshly ground black pepper

1 Cook the pasta following the
instructions in the introduction.

2 ▲ Melt the butter in a large frying
pan and fry the garlic and mushrooms
for about 5 minutes until browned and
the liquid from the mushrooms has
evaporated.

3 Take the mushrooms out of the pan
and remove the pan from the heat. Stir
in the flour, then add the milk until it is
absorbed by the flour.

4 Return the pan to the heat and stir in
the Parmesan, fontina and ricotta
cheeses and bring almost to a boil. Add
the cream and chives. Season to taste.

5 Drain the pasta and place it in a large
serving bowl. Pour over the sauce and
toss to coat. Serve immediately.

COOK'S TIP

*You can use any type of mushroom in this
sauce. Italians would use porcini because
of their pronounced taste and because they
do not lose their texture when cooked. If
you can't find fresh porcini, or cep, Italian
grocery stores always sell the dried variety.*

Pasta Rounds with Parmesan Sauce

*This is an extremely quick and simple
sauce, perfect for those in a hurry.*

SERVES 4

INGREDIENTS

1 lb pasta rounds (castiglioni)
¼ cup butter
1¼ cups heavy cream
1 cup Parmesan cheese, freshly grated
salt and freshly ground black pepper
2 tbsp pine nuts, toasted
*finely shredded fresh flat leaf parsley,
to garnish*

1 Cook the pasta following the
instructions in the introduction.

2 ▲ Heat the butter and cream
together in a saucepan.

3 ▲ Stir in half the Parmesan cheese
and heat gently, stirring occasionally.
Keep the sauce warm.

4 Drain the pasta and turn it into a
large serving bowl. Stir in the
remaining Parmesan cheese and
seasoning until coated. Pour over the
sauce and toss to coat. Sprinkle on the
pine nuts and serve immediately,
garnished with parsley.

*Tortellini with Mushroom and Three
Cheese Sauce (top), and Pasta Rounds
with Parmesan Sauce (bottom).*

Pasta Spirals with Lentil and Cheese Sauce

SERVES 4

INGREDIENTS

12 oz pasta spirals (fusilli)
1 tbsp olive oil
1 onion, chopped
1 garlic clove, chopped
1 carrot, cut into matchsticks
½ cup green lentils, boiled for
 25 minutes
1 tbsp tomato paste
1 tbsp chopped fresh oregano
⅔ cup vegetable stock
1⅓ cups Cheddar cheese, freshly
 grated
salt and freshly ground black pepper
freshly grated cheese, to serve

1 ▲ Heat the oil in a large frying pan and fry the onion and garlic for 3 minutes. Add the carrot and cook for a further 5 minutes.

2 Cook the pasta following the instructions in the introduction.

3 ▲ Stir the lentils, tomato paste and oregano into the frying pan, cover and cook for 3 minutes.

4 ▲ Add the stock, and salt and pepper to the pan, cover and simmer for 10 minutes. Add the cheese.

5 Drain the pasta thoroughly and stir it into the sauce to coat. Serve with plenty of extra grated cheese.

COOK'S TIP

Tomato purée is sold in small cans and tubes. If you use a can for this small amount, you can keep the remainder fresh by transferring it to a bowl, covering it with a thin layer of olive oil and putting it in the fridge.

Penne with Gorgonzola Sauce

*Pasta tossed in a rich, creamy sauce is
ideal to serve for an evening meal.*

SERVES 4

INGREDIENTS
*1 lb penne
¼ cup butter
1 onion, chopped
2 celery stalks, chopped
1 garlic clove, chopped
1 tbsp chopped fresh basil (optional)
1 cup light cream
¾ cup gorgonzola cheese, grated
1⅓ cup mascarpone cheese
salt and freshly ground black
    pepper
poppy seeds, to garnish (optional)*

1 Cook the pasta following the
instructions in the introduction.

2 ▲ Melt the butter in a frying pan and
fry the onion, celery and garlic over a
gentle heat for about 10 minutes until
softened, stirring occasionally. Stir in
the basil and cream and heat through.

3 ▲ Pour the vegetable mixture into a
food processor or blender and blend
until smooth.

4 Pour the sauce into the pan and
bring almost to a boil, stirring
occasionally. Add the gorgonzola,
mascarpone, salt and pepper. Heat
gently until the cheeses melt.

5 Drain the pasta thoroughly. Stir it
into the sauce, tossing well to coat.
Serve immediately, garnished with
poppy seeds.

COOK'S TIP

*Gorgonzola is a semi-soft blue-veined
cheese with quite a strong flavour made in
the Lombardy region of Italy. It should be
creamy yellow with irregular blue veining.
Do not purchase any if it is hard or has a
bitter smell.*

Spaghetti with Eggplant and Tomato Sauce

A recipe for a supper menu – serve this eggplant and tomato dish with freshly cooked snow peas.

SERVES 4

INGREDIENTS
3 small eggplants
salt and freshly ground black pepper
olive oil, for frying
1 lb spaghetti
1 quantity Classic Tomato Sauce (see Curly Lasagne with Classic Tomato Sauce)
1¹/₃ cups fontina cheese, grated

I Top and tail the eggplants and slice them thinly.

2 ▲ Arrange the eggplant slices in a colander, sprinkling with plenty of salt between each layer. Place the colander over a plate and let stand for about 30 minutes.

3 ▲ Rinse the eggplants under cold running water. Drain thoroughly and pat dry with paper towels.

4 ▲ Heat plenty of oil in a large frying pan and fry the eggplant slices in batches for about 5 minutes, turning once during cooking until browned.

5 Meanwhile, cook the pasta following the instructions in the introduction.

6 ▲ Stir the tomato sauce into the pan with the eggplants and bring to a boil. Cover and simmer for 5 minutes.

7 ▲ Stir in the fontina cheese and salt and pepper and continue stirring over a medium heat until the cheese melts.

8 Drain the pasta and stir into the sauce, tossing well to coat.

COOK'S TIP

Supermarkets and specialist delicatessens sell hybrid baby eggplants that are ideal for using in this sauce. They are available year round. If you use these, they will brown in 3–5 minutes in step 4.

Pasta Twists with Cream and Cheese Sauce

SERVES 4

INGREDIENTS
12 oz pasta twists (spirali)
2 tbsp butter
1 onion, chopped
1 garlic clove, chopped
1 tbsp chopped fresh oregano
1¼ cups sour cream
½ cup mozzarella cheese, grated
½ cup Bel Paese cheese, grated
5 sun-dried tomatoes in oil, drained
*   and sliced*
salt and freshly ground black
*   pepper*

I Cook the pasta following the instructions in the introduction.

2 ▲ Melt the butter in a large frying pan and fry the onion for 10 minutes until softened. Add the garlic and cook for 1 minute.

COOK'S TIP

Finely chop the leftover oregano leaves and store in a jar of extra-virgin olive oil, ready to use in salad dressings or other pasta sauces.

3 ▲ Stir in the oregano and cream and heat gently until almost boiling. Stir in the mozzarella and Bel Paese cheeses and heat gently, stirring occasionally until melted. Add the sun-dried tomatoes and season to taste.

4 Drain the pasta and turn it into a serving bowl. Pour over the sauce and toss well to coat. Serve immediately.

Short Pasta Tubes with Cheese and Coriander Sauce

A speedy supper dish, this is best served with a tomato and basil salad.

SERVES 4

INGREDIENTS
1 lb short pasta tubes (canneroni)
4 oz/⅔ cup garlic and herb cheese
2 tbsp minced fresh coriander
1¼ cups light cream
salt and freshly ground black pepper
1 cup green peas, cooked

I Cook the pasta following the instructions in the introduction.

2 ▲ Melt the cheese in a small pan over a low heat until smooth.

3 Stir in the coriander, cream, and salt and pepper. Bring slowly to a boil, stirring occasionally until well blended. Stir in the peas and continue cooking until heated through.

4 Drain the pasta and turn it into a large serving bowl. Pour over the sauce and toss to coat thoroughly.

COOK'S TIP

If you do not like the pronounced flavour of fresh coriander substitute another fresh herb, such as basil or flat leaf parsley.

Pasta Twists with Cream and Cheese Sauce (top), and Short Pasta Tubes with Cheese and Coriander Sauce (bottom).

Sauces for Special Occasions

You only have to go to an Italian delicatessen to see the range of authentic ingredients and delicacies that can be added to pasta sauces. In this chapter, I have used unusual ingredients that may cost more but will make your meal that much more special. Once you start experimenting with different combinations of ingredients you can create feasts fit for any occasion.

Above   Grain sacks at Padua market.

Opposite   Portofino, Liguria.

Tagliatelle with Smoked Salmon, Cucumber and Dill Sauce

This is a pretty pasta sauce with the light texture of the cucumber complementing the fish perfectly.

SERVES 4

INGREDIENTS
12 oz tagliatelle
1/2 cucumber
6 tbsp butter
grated rind of 1 orange
2 tbsp chopped fresh dill
1 1/4 cups light cream
2/3 cup orange juice
salt and freshly ground black pepper
4 oz smoked salmon

1 Cook the pasta following the instructions in the introduction.

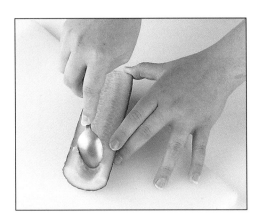

2 ▲ Using a sharp knife, cut the cucumber in half lengthways, then using a small spoon scoop out the cucumber seeds and discard.

3 ▲ Turn the cucumber on the flat side and slice it thinly.

4 ▲ Melt the butter in a saucepan, add the orange rind and dill and stir well. Add the cucumber and cook gently for about 2 minutes, stirring occasionally.

5 ▲ Add the cream, orange juice and seasoning and simmer for 1 minute.

6 ▲ Meanwhile, cut the salmon into thin strips.

7 ▲ Stir the salmon into the sauce and heat through.

8 Drain the pasta thoroughly and toss it in the sauce. Serve immediately.

COOK'S TIP

An economical way to make this sauce for a special occasion is to use smoked salmon bits, sold in most delicatessens and some supermarkets. Smoked trout is a less expensive alternative.

Pasta Twists with Wild Mushroom and Chorizo Sauce

The delicious combination of wild mushrooms and spicy sausage make this a tempting evening supper dish.

SERVES 4

INGREDIENTS

12 oz pasta twists (spirali)
4 tbsp olive oil
1 garlic clove, chopped
1 celery stalk, chopped
8 oz chorizo sausage, sliced
3 cups mixed mushrooms, such as oyster,
*   cremini, shiitake*
1 tbsp lemon juice
2 tbsp chopped fresh oregano
salt and freshly ground black pepper
finely chopped fresh parsley, to garnish

1 Cook the pasta following the instructions in the introduction.

2 ▲ Heat the oil in a frying pan and cook the garlic and celery for 5 minutes until the celery is softened.

3 ▲ Add the chorizo and cook for 5 minutes, stirring occasionally until browned.

4 ▲ Add the mushrooms and cook for a further 4 minutes, stirring occasionally until slightly softened.

5 ▲ Stir in the remaining ingredients, except the garnish, and heat through.

6 ▲ Drain the pasta thoroughly and turn it into a serving bowl. Toss with the sauce to coat. Serve immediately, garnished with fresh parsley.

COOK'S TIP

This dish is delicious served with lots of Parmesan cheese shavings. Use any combination of mushrooms for this flavorful sauce.

Pasta Tubes with Scallop Sauce

A jewel from the sea such as scallop is what makes this sauce so special. Serve with a light green salad.

SERVES 4

INGREDIENTS
12 oz pasta tubes (rigatoni)
12 oz sea scallops
3 tbsp olive oil
1 garlic clove, chopped
1 onion, chopped
2 carrots, cut into matchsticks
2 tbsp chopped fresh parsley
2 tbsp dry white wine
2 tbsp Pernod
²/₃ cup heavy cream
salt and freshly ground black pepper

1 Cook the pasta following the instructions in the introduction.

2 ▲ Trim the scallops, separating the corals from the white eye part of meat.

3 ▲ Using a sharp knife, cut the eye in half lengthways.

4 ▲ Heat the oil in a frying pan and fry the garlic, onion and carrots for 5–10 minutes until the carrots are softened.

5 ▲ Stir in the scallops, parsley, wine and Pernod and bring to the boil. Cover and simmer for about 1 minute. Using a slotted spoon, transfer the scallops and vegetables to a plate and keep them warm.

6 ▲ Bring the pan juices back to the boil and boil rapidly until reduced by half. Stir in the cream and heat the sauce through.

7 ▲ Return the scallops and vegetables to the pan and heat through. Season the mixture to taste.

8 Drain the pasta thoroughly and toss it with the sauce. Serve immediately.

COOK'S TIP

The key to this sauce is not to overcook the scallops in step 2, or they will become tough and rubbery. Frozen scallops look pure white, while fresh scallops have a creamy-grey color.

Linguine with Smoked Ham and Artichoke Sauce

SERVES 4

INGREDIENTS

12 oz linguine
3 tbsp olive oil
1 onion, chopped
2 cloves garlic, chopped
14 oz can artichokes, drained and
*   sliced*
1 1/3 cups Virginia smoked ham,
*   diced*
2 tbsp chopped fresh basil
1 tbsp herb vinegar
salt and freshly ground black pepper
2/3 cup sour cream
fresh mint sprigs, to garnish

I Cook the pasta following the instructions in the introduction.

2 ▲ Heat the oil in a frying pan and fry the onion and garlic for 5 minutes. Add the artichokes.

COOK'S TIP

Use boiled ham if you prefer. Smoked chicken is also delicious in this recipe.

3 ▲ Cook the artichokes for 2 minutes, then add the ham and basil and fry, stirring, for 2 minutes. Add the herb vinegar and seasoning and heat through. Stir in the cream and heat through again.

4 Drain the pasta thoroughly and toss it with the sauce. Serve immediately, garnished with fresh mint.

Penne with Anchovy and Broccoli Sauce

SERVES 4

INGREDIENTS

12 oz penne
4 tbsp olive oil
1 clove garlic, chopped
1 red onion, chopped
2 tbsp pine nuts
2 oz can anchovies
1 1/2 cups broccoli florets
salt and freshly ground black pepper

COOK'S TIP

Anchovies are very salty, so for those who don't like too much salt, soak the anchovies in milk for 30 minutes before chopping. Taste the sauce before seasoning.

I Cook the pasta following the instructions in the introduction.

2 Heat the oil in a saucepan and fry the garlic, onion and pine nuts for 5 minutes until softened.

3 ▲ Chop the anchovies and stir into the onion mixture, including the oil from the tin. Cook gently for 1 minute, mashing the anchovies slightly with the back of a wooden spoon.

4 ▲ Stir in the broccoli, cover and simmer for 5 minutes until the broccoli is tender. Stir in the seasoning.

5 Drain the pasta thoroughly and toss it in the sauce. Serve immediately.

Linguine with Smoked Ham and Artichoke Sauce (top), and Penne with Anchovy and Broccoli Sauce (bottom).

Tagliatelle with Prosciutto, Asparagus and Cheese Sauce

A stunning sauce, this is worth every effort to serve for a special occasion evening meal.

SERVES 4

INGREDIENTS
12 oz tagliatelle
2 tbsp butter
1 tbsp olive oil
8 oz asparagus tips
1 garlic clove, chopped
4 oz prosciutto, sliced into strips
2 tbsp chopped fresh sage
⅔ cup light cream
4 oz/⅔ cup chive-and-onion double Gloucester cheese, grated
⅔ cup Gruyère cheese, grated
salt and freshly ground black pepper
fresh sage sprigs, to garnish

1 Cook the pasta following the instructions in the introduction.

2 ▲ Melt the butter and oil in a frying pan and gently fry the asparagus tips for about 5 minutes, stirring occasionally until almost tender.

3 ▲ Stir in the garlic and prosciutto and fry for 1 minute.

4 ▲ Stir in the sage leaves and fry for 1 minute more.

5 ▲ Pour in the cream and bring to the boil.

6 ▲ Add the cheeses and simmer gently, stirring occasionally until thoroughly melted. Season to taste.

7 ▲ Drain the pasta thoroughly and toss it with the sauce to coat. Serve immediately, garnished with fresh sage.

Linguine with Sweet Pepper and Cream Sauce

SERVES 4

INGREDIENTS
1 orange pepper, cored and quartered
1 yellow pepper, cored and quartered
1 red pepper, cored and quartered
12 oz linguine
2 tbsp olive oil
1 red onion, sliced
1 garlic clove, chopped
2 tbsp chopped fresh rosemary
²/₃ cup heavy cream
salt and freshly ground black pepper
fresh rosemary sprigs, to garnish

I Preheat the broiler.

2 ▲ Place the peppers skin sides up on a broiling pan. Broil for 5–10 minutes until the pepper skins begin to blister and char.

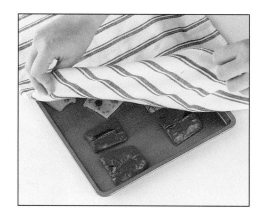

3 ▲ Remove the peppers from the heat, cover with a clean dish towel and let stand for 5 minutes.

4 ▲ Carefully peel away the skins from the peppers and discard. Slice the peppers into thin strips.

5 Cook the pasta following the instructions in the introduction.

6 ▲ Heat the oil in a frying pan and fry the onion and garlic for about 5 minutes until softened.

7 ▲ Stir in the peppers and rosemary and fry gently for about 5 minutes until heated through.

8 ▲ Stir in the cream and heat through gently. Season to taste.

9 Drain the pasta thoroughly and toss in the sauce. Serve immediately, garnished with fresh rosemary.

COOK'S TIP

Be sure to char the pepper skins all over for easy skinning. If you have a gas burner, spear the peppers whole and hold them over the flame until they are charred.

Mixed Summer Pasta

A pretty colorful sauce with lots of flavor makes this a dish for the summer.

SERVES 4

INGREDIENTS
12 oz curly spaghetti (fusilli col buco)
4 oz green beans, cut into 1 in pieces
salt and freshly ground black pepper
2 tbsp olive oil
½ fennel bulb, sliced
1 bunch scallions, sliced diagonally
4 oz yellow cherry tomatoes
4 oz red cherry tomatoes
2 tbsp chopped fresh dill
8 oz peeled shrimp
1 tbsp lemon juice
1 tbsp wholegrain mustard
4 tbsp sour cream
fresh dill sprigs, to garnish

I ▲ Cook the beans in boiling salted water for about 5 minutes until tender, then drain.

2 Cook the pasta following the instructions in the introduction.

3 ▲ Heat the oil in a frying pan and fry the fennel and scallions for about 5 minutes.

4 ▲ Stir in the cherry tomatoes and fry for a further 5 minutes, stirring occasionally.

5 ▲ Add the dill and shrimp and cook for 1 minute.

6 ▲ Stir in the lemon juice, mustard, sour cream, seasoning and beans and simmer for 1 minute.

7 Drain the pasta and toss with the sauce. Serve immediately, garnished with fresh dill.

COOK'S TIP

Yellow cherry tomatoes are not always in season, so simply substitute red cherry tomatoes.

Index